Praise for *TOUGH TALK*

"Anyone in business can identify with some, if not all, of the scenarios in *Tough Talk*. Becky and Andrea have concisely laid out practical steps specific to each scenario that will improve your chances of getting a positive outcome. Perhaps more importantly, their straightforward discussion on the necessity of preparation for any difficult talk situation, whether business or personal, is extremely helpful and will be beneficial to all who use the preparation framework."

Josh Coughlin, Chief Executive Officer & President
Benovus Bio, Inc.

"*Tough Talk* is a practical tool for anyone dealing with difficult conversations and situations. It provides a great framework for planning and practice."

Lucinda Smith, SVP, Global Business Services
AGCO Corporation

"*Tough Talk* has great insight and tips that we can build into our everyday conversations. I am thrilled with how Andrea and Becky wrote this book—it reminded me of how many areas of our work touch areas where we could be faced with critical conversations. I encourage everyone who reads *Tough Talk* to complete the exercises —write down your experiences, goals, and follow the guidelines—then

Praise for *TOUGH TALK*

share them with a friend or colleague. I did it! And I learned even more about how I, as a women leader in business, can become better prepared and more aware of how to have a tough talk."

Lisa Schneider, Director, Operations, Government and Healthcare, W.W. Grainger, Inc.

"Becky and Andrea have addressed the core elements of tough discussions while providing a great guide for managers and team members who want to interact at a higher level of honesty. The result of implementing the tips in *Tough Talk* will be a stronger, more committed team—one that is prepared to operate in an atmosphere promoting direct communication."

Dr. Edward Shellard, Chief Marketing Officer & Director of Business Development, Carestream Health, Inc.

"This is a solid book that I heartily recommend. It's a fast read with insights and tips that are easily implemented. For the experienced manager or the newly graduated, tough conversations are a business reality. *Tough Talk* provides the framework and ideas on how to make those conversations productive and successful. I think their advice, 'Be proactive. Be bold. Be prepared. Go first.' is spot on and a terrific rallying point for people to lean into their discomfort about tackling tough issues."

Bill Gentner, SVP, Chief Marketing Officer Stage Stores

Praise for *TOUGH TALK*

"I applaud *Tough Talk* for providing very clear and pragmatic advice that both employees and leaders can apply. It also includes a terrific collection of memorable quotes that capture the essence of effective communication! Too often, books of this nature are targeted at management. Employees are left with minimal tools and tips to help them address challenges they face on a regular basis. *Tough Talk* does an excellent job of providing very accessible tips for both populations.

"Clearwater Consulting did great work helping our newly formed executive team get clear on the culture we are trying to create and "naming the agreements" most critical for our ongoing success (Tip #5). I highly recommend them for work with teams and individuals."

**Thana Sakas, Vice President, Talent Asset Management
Benchmark Brands, Inc.**

"I have worked with Becky and Andrea for many years. *Tough Talk* is the beginning and the end on how to effectively tackle tough conversations in the workplace. These 10 tips are the guardrails I consistently follow when tackling tough issues in the workplace. My communication, negotiation, and leadership skills have all been enhanced because of the lessons laid out beautifully in this book. These 10 tips are a must have for anyone in the workplace who wants to lead at a high level."

**Josh Bergman, VP
Macy's**

Praise for *TOUGH TALK*

"At the heart of this book is the simple truth—disarming difficult situations begins with our own preparation. In *Tough Talk*, Becky and Andrea discuss 10 of the most common situations and provide keen insight and practical steps to approach your most difficult situation or person. After reading the book, I was inspired to tackle my most difficult situation with confidence and with a concrete plan for success."

Trish Coughlin, President
Peachtree Medical Consultants, Inc.

"Chefs have known how to turn 'tough into tender' for centuries. Business leaders now have the opportunity to do the same. Clearwater has led our senior leadership team through numerous difficult situations over the years. It's amazing how they can take a seemingly impossible event and turn it into a collaborative solution."

John Deushane, President & General Manager
WXIA/WATL, Gannett

"As an attorney who works with executives in 'involuntary transition,' I know that very few of us—aside perhaps from the extroverts in outside sales—desire to repeatedly engage in professional reinvention. Involuntary transitions have a multi-factor etiology. They tend to share both a blindness to perception and a gradual breakdown of communications. Given the choice between having a difficult conversation or having none at all, we all too often kick the can down the road. Sooner or later, we find ourselves on an altogether

Praise for *TOUGH TALK*

different road, only to discover that geographical changes rarely result in a remedy for what truly ails us.

"With *Tough Talk*, Andrea Hopke and Becky Dannenfelser chart a different course. They urge us to recognize the elephant in the room and to confront it here and now, strategically, thoughtfully, and effectively. They offer unique tools for both introspection and communication that should be on the hip of every executive who hopes to claim a leadership role within a corporation, institution, or organization."

Kevin D. Fitzpatrick, Jr.
DeLong, Caldwell, Bridgers & Fitzpatrick

"Reading *Tough Talk* makes me think of an NFL quarterback approaching the line and reading the defense. Depending on what he sees as the situation with the person on the other side, he can use one of the nine plays on his armband (Run DISC, 360, etc.) to reach a successful outcome. If the quarterback does not recognize what is being presented, then he can call a timeout, go to the sideline and get help from his coach. Thanks for designing the armband tool that outlines which is the correct play to run depending on the situation and for providing assistance when I needed to call a timeout."

Bruce Yeager, Managing Consultant
Viscadia, Inc.

> *In organizations,
> real power and energy are
> generated through relationships.
> The patterns of relationships and
> the capacities to form them are
> more important than tasks,
> functions, roles, and positions.*
>
> Margaret Wheatley

TOUGH TALK

Ten Tips for Disarming Difficult Conversations

Andrea Hopke & Becky Dannenfelser
Clearwater Consulting Group, Inc.

Copyright © 2014 Andrea Hopke & Becky Dannenfelser

All rights reserved. No part of this book may be reproduced in any form or by any electronic or mechanical means including information storage and retrieval systems—except in the case of brief quotations embodied in critical articles or reviews—without permission in writing from Andrea Hopke and Becky Dannenfelser.

ISBN: 978-0-9916085-0-8

This book may be purchased in bulk for educational, business, fundraising or sales promotional use. For information please contact:
    Andrea Hopke, andrea@clearwater-consulting.com
    Becky Dannenfelser, becky@clearwater-consulting.com
    www.clearwater-consulting.com
    404-634-4332

Cover and interior layout design by: Vanessa Lowry
Photography by: Brooke Kremer
Editing by: Dr. Tim Morrison

Printed by BookLogix Publishing Services, Alpharetta, GA

TOUGH TALK
Dedication

For our courageous clients who step up to tackle tough conversations.

And for our husbands, Steve and Mark, on whom we have had ample opportunity to practice these tips.

> *It was impossible to get a conversation going, everyone was talking too much.*
>
> Yogi Berra

TOUGH TALK
Table of Contents

Foreword 1

Introduction 5

Chapter 1: Critical Performance Reviews 9

Chapter 2: Negotiations 17

Chapter 3: Poor Leadership 23

Chapter 4: Lack of Career Advancement 33

Chapter 5: Confronting Abrasive Behavior 39

Chapter 6: Executive Presence 47

Chapter 7: Change Resistant 55

Chapter 8: Apologizing 63

Chapter 9: Peer-to-Peer Accountability 71

Chapter 10: Preparing For A Difficult Conversation 79

Conclusion 93

Endnotes 97

About Clearwater Consulting 101

About the Authors 111

> *Life is 10% what happens to you and 90% how you react to it.*
>
> Lou Holtz

TOUGH TALK
Foreword

In my business life, I have engaged in a variety of complex situations including managing global organizations with language and cultural challenges, as well as starting companies from scratch and taking a company public. As you can imagine, I have tackled tough talk in many of those situations, and continue to do so today.

What I appreciate about the approach offered in *Tough Talk* is its collection of simple yet practical techniques with little "consultant speak." I've learned that simplicity, practical thinking, and methodology work far better than the incredible complexity many consultants design to create a greater illusion of value. We don't need to make it more difficult than it is. Many of us become so overwhelmed by the "game plan" that we can't even enter the arena.

My favorite quote in this book is, "The person who can most accurately describe reality without laying blame will emerge the leader." This illustrates the point that someone who can understand the situation in which they find themselves—and articulate it in such a way that diffuses defensiveness—will negate the confrontational and emotional response many of us fall into.

Tough talk does not need to imply uncomfortable confrontation. As noted in this book, there are many ways to handle these situations without the need to be a "pit bull." I find kindness and sincerity work better—even with the "toughest" of individuals. A calm confidence usually disarms the screamer.

What *Tough Talk* encourages is developing skills to gain that calm confidence rather than teaching hand-to-hand combat. It also points to the essential quality of self-awareness, knowing who we are and what we bring to the conversation, including a desire to understand the other person.

A common misunderstanding is that tough situations require "tough talk"—which is presumed to mean being tough. This paralyzes many people because they think only toughness wins and they're not capable of that. A "win/win" attitude will ALWAYS produce better results. While maybe not in the immediate short term, certainly better results over time.

I have learned the painful lesson that completely getting your way in negotiations will feel good in the short term, but will eventually lead to a cost (usually manifested in lack of cooperation from the other party when you need something from them). Relationships matter in negotiations, as much as talent and negotiating techniques. A win/lose mentality does not instill trust and few relationships, partnerships, or alliances last without trust.

Don't misunderstand me. Winning isn't always easy and life certainly isn't always "fair." However, those of us who invest the time and energy into developing our personal skills—and are willing to treat others as we would like to be treated—have a tremendous advantage in navigating through the issues we will inevitably face. *Tough Talk* can assist you in developing those skills.

Dan Myers, President/CEO, Alimera Sciences

*Sensitivity to others is no trivial skill; rather, it is a truly precious human ability.
But it isn't complex: it requires receptiveness to other people and a willingness to listen.*

James Kouzes & Barry Posner

TOUGH TALK
Introduction

It happened again. Your colleague missed the deadline, which means you will miss your deadline. Again. What should you do?

Or, your boss is repeatedly adding new projects for your team without clearly prioritizing existing ones or helping you understand how this work fits with the other initiatives. How do you raise a red flag without risking her high regard of you as capable of handling anything that arises?

Perhaps you need to deliver a less than positive performance review for an employee. This is someone you know is introverted and quiet, but you need him to be more assertive in meetings with peers from other departments; otherwise, they think he is not competent and the entire department suffers. What should you do?

This book talks about those challenging conversations and more. It offers practical tips for building your confidence through preparation and insight about yourself and others. Most of us do not believe we are skilled at tackling tough conversations. We delay until the situation festers and no amount of diplomacy can save us. Given that the need to have challenging conversations is pervasive, whether with a peer, a manager, a direct report or board member, it is about time we each took responsibility for developing the skill. [1]

Why are we all so bad at this? Studies indicate: none of us is skilled at either seeking or providing feedback or input on a regular basis. It doesn't matter if it is a formal setting such as a performance review or an informal conversation. And what we do not enjoy, we avoid. We ignore. We postpone.

Disagreements or conflicting views can occur in any direction—with your superiors, with your peers or colleagues, with your direct reports or staff, or with your customers and clients. John Maxwell, author of *The 360 Degree Leader*, frames this really well in terms of 'up,' 'across,' and 'down' from wherever you sit in the company. And no matter what your position within the organization, you play a role in creating a culture in which directness, candor, problem solving and resolution can occur.

And what about gender differences? Women do view difficult conversations differently from their male counterparts. Research suggests that women tend to fall into particular ruts. Women avoid or over-accommodate, leading to regret or frustration. But even more, there is a fiscal impact:

women may leave on the table between $1 million and $1.5 million in revenue due to lack of negotiation skills. [2]

Men may avoid challenging conversations because they fear an emotional response from a woman. Interestingly, roughly eight of ten men feel the need to be careful and indirect in providing feedback to women while eight of ten women want direct feedback. [3]

This book is designed to share our insights and tips for tackling the most prevalent difficult conversations and how best to prepare for them. Collectively, all ten tips apply to any challenging situation. We start from the premise that you have both the responsibility and control over how you respond to a situation and we want you to be well informed before you do. If you read nothing else in this book, read Tip 10: Be prepared. Other than that, there is no particular order to the chapters, so find one that speaks to a current theme in your life and check it out today.

> You have both the responsibility and control over how you respond to a situation.

The single biggest problem with communication is the illusion that it has taken place.

George Bernard Shaw

DIFFICULT CONVERSATION #1
Critical Performance Reviews

Performance reviews, especially ones that offer a critical view of the employee, are challenging to deliver and painful to receive. What is the root cause of this anguish?

From our perspective, there are several elements: lack of clear goals which tie to organizational strategy, lack of commitment on the part of the employee, lack of support on the part of the manager, no feedback or input throughout the year so it is delivered as a once-a-year hammer. We have trained ourselves that performance reviews are more likely to be critical rather than supportive. So we avoid, delay, or drop and run—anything to avoid the pain of delivery. And, heaven forbid, we should be proactive and ASK for input or feedback!

Yet, therein lays the answer: responsibility rests on both sides of the table.

As a manager, how proactive are you about helping your direct reports establish meaningful goals? Goals lay the foundation for evaluating other's performance. Do you know what success looks like? As simple as that sounds, we see many companies and managers struggling with the basic maneuver of articulating goals and clearly defining outcomes. Goals could include establishing a revenue achievement, management skill development, or specific behavior change. For example, with the escalating need for greater collaboration given increasingly interdependent work within teams and across organizations,[4] how might you define the behaviors of collaboration so you (and the employee) are very clear what it is and isn't?

Hopefully, both the manager and the employee contribute to the initial conversation about what is possible and about what each will commit to doing in order to achieve success. The manager agrees to provide coaching, training, resources, and ongoing input. The employee creates a plan to address areas needing to be strengthened and seeks input on a regular basis so there are no surprises at year end. One of the most challenging disconnects we see is even when expectations are established, manager and employee do not revisit them periodically. Instead, assumptions rule the day rather than clarity—the employee assumes the manager knows where he is on the project; the manager assumes the employee is on target.

As someone who is being evaluated, how adept are you at tracking your own performance against the established goals? How proactive are you at getting input along the way? Will you commit to establishing the goal of delivering (or receiving) performance feedback more regularly?

The truth is most of us fail miserably at creating a plan for tackling what needs to change. That simple step of creating a plan alleviates many ongoing issues by bringing clarity to expectations and defining the specific, measurable behaviors or outcomes both employee and manager agree to support. In the absence of a plan for addressing a particular behavior change or targeted accomplishment, the work of the day consumes us. We quickly fail to move toward the desired goal. [5]

> Responsibility rests on both sides of the table.

TIP #1

Tough Self-Talk - Focus on your own improvement

What is a recurrent theme in your feedback sessions or in any assessments you have received? What is one specific area you know you could improve, one over which you have control?

- Craft a brief, practical plan with specific milestones and a list of resources to ensure development of the stated goal.

- Create a 90-day timeline to improve in that particular area. Share it with a colleague for initial input.

- Schedule time with your boss to seek their input. The simple act of being proactive helps you stand out, shows that you take initiative, are motivated, and committed.

CHAPTER 1: Critical Performance Review

Write down two to three milestones to which you are committed in the next 90 days.

TOUGH TALK – Ten Tips for Disarming Difficult Conversations

*Everyone you meet
is your mirror.*

Ken Keyes Jr.

Women are not as good negotiating for themselves as men are, mostly because of different expectations. But women outperform men in representational negotiations—that is, negotiating for someone else.

Margaret A. Neale

DIFFICULT CONVERSATION #2
Negotiations

Probably THE most difficult conversation around negotiations regards salary. But there are others—job definition, work life balance, time off, hours, getting promoted. Recent research from Salary.com reports in their blog, "Most People Don't Negotiate Due to Fear and Lack of Skills." In addition, we avoid negotiating because of perceived unpleasantness or lack of confidence.[6]

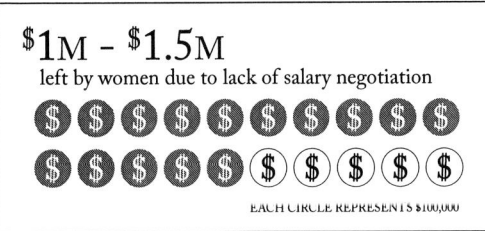

Gender does matter when it comes to negotiation. Women are actually better than men in representing others in negotiations.[7] But men are four times more likely to negotiate a salary increase for themselves compared to women, according to Linda Babcock in her book, *Women Don't Ask*. This lack of negotiation among women can be costly, with an estimated one million to $1.5 million left on the table, per Babcock.[2] But, women are not the only ones who leave money on the table. An estimated 18% of the population never negotiate salary, costing themselves a minimum of $500,000 by the time they reach sixty.[6]

What can help prepare you for the tough topic of salary increase or job clarity or getting promoted? Margaret A. Neale, a professor at Stanford, teaches a four-step negotiation process that helps individuals overcome their fear or lack of skills:[8]

1. **Assess.** Some of the questions Dr. Neale raises are: "Do the benefits of engaging in this negotiation outweigh the costs? Can you have influence in this situation? What is the price you are willing to pay to avoid negotiating?"

2. **Prepare.** (See chapter 10 later in this book.)

3. **Ask.** She suggests we think about the interaction as an opportunity to share information and points to the importance of asking them for their perspective.

4. **Package.** By this she means to propose a package of solutions (versus negotiating one item at a time).

CHAPTER 2: Negotiations

TIP #2

Know what you are worth

To package your proposal for a salary conversation, get the data you need. Go to the salary wizard on Salary.com to get some perspective of your dollar value based on a comparison of other similar roles.

> Men are four times more likely than women to negotiate a salary increase.

Identify one thing to do today that will help prepare you for the tough topic of salary increase, job clarity, or getting promoted.

CHAPTER 2: Negotiations

*The truth will set you free—
but first it may
thoroughly irritate you.*

Susan Scott

DIFFICULT CONVERSATION #3
Poor Leadership

Poor leadership can happen at any level—your boss, your peers, your direct reports. The toughest conversation, however, is with your boss.

You have at least 3 choices:

1. Ignore it, hoping that someone else will tackle your boss with the truth; unfortunately, given the research on how we all avoid difficult conversations and how bad we are at them, this is unlikely. And you'll soon leave because the lack of integrity of working for a poor leader will begin to weigh on you. In the late 1990s, Buckingham and Coffman first pointed to the fact that people left managers, not companies.

2. Suggest to your boss or to HR that your entire team, including your boss, go through a 360 degree evaluation process, so that everyone gets input at the same time and can benefit for

a team-wide experience of learning, sharing, and committing to necessary changes. (For suggestions on various 360 degree approaches, check out our website: www.clearwater-consulting.com)

3. Be brave and have the difficult conversation with your boss, but prepare well for it (see Tip 10) by focusing on what you need, not on what is wrong with him or her. You love your job, you love the company, you want to succeed here—but your manager shows lack of direction: there is no clarity, no apparent vision about where the department is headed or how it fits into the organizational strategy; she isn't fighting for what the team needs; he did not involve the team the last time a major decision was made, he shares no credit for successes. The list is long. Pick one that matters most to you, then prepare by talking about what you need in order to succeed.

A limiting perspective we run into from time to time is the belief that people really cannot change. This was true of a client who was convinced he was next in line for a huge promotion. In an interesting turn of events, Tom's boss sat him down one day after a major international presentation to the Senior Leaders of the company and said, "You need to change. We love the work you produce and your obsession with

CHAPTER 3: Poor Leadership

getting stellar results, but you tick people off at every step. You do not know how to partner with others. There were six people up there on your team who were supposed to play a role in that presentation, and all we heard was 'I' from you. You think you are going to be promoted and you aren't. We cannot have an arrogant, senior vice president even if you do hit it out of the park." She offered him the chance to work with an executive coach.

Tough talk for a manager to hear, especially for one who had always been told he had high potential and was going to go far. Sure, he had had some of this feedback along the way, but he ignored it, using as the excuse "It's just the way I am. Blunt, brash, confident. People don't change!" Tom even thought about leaving and not putting himself through the painful process, but our Clearwater Consulting coach convinced him, "This behavior will follow you to the next company if you don't deal with it now."

Our client was introduced to the 360 degree feedback process through which his peers, his boss, other senior leaders, and his direct reports shared confidential observations about our client's work style, his communication habits, and delivery of work. As his Clearwater Consulting coach reviewed the report with him, some of it stunning in its bluntness, she refused to let him excuse any of the abrasive behavior, inviting him instead to consider:

- What role do you want to play in repairing relationships with—your boss, peers and direct reports? How many people have you offended at each level?

- As outstanding as your results have been, what impact will positive relationships with more collaboration have on your results? How will this collaboration and leverage of the repaired relationships move your +38% to potentially +50%?

- What do people need to hear from you that will convince them you are committed to a new way of operating at work?

Our work lasted a year with this client. We are happy to say, he made all the changes necessary to re-position himself at this organization—rising to a senior role with a large team and a lot of responsibility.

> Discard the limiting belief that people can't change.

TIP #3

Ask for it—Conduct 360 Degree Feedback on Yourself

360 Degree Feedback is the process of inviting your manager, your peers, and your direct reports to provide information about how they perceive you on key elements or dimensions important to your work and to your success.

- If your company has a formal process or program for completing a 360, ask that your team participate.

- If the company does not, then sponsor the project yourself. Identify eight to ten people whose opinion you respect. Create a short list of questions you would like them to answer, including these: what are my strengths; what one thing can I start doing today that would improve my positive impact; how would you describe my "brand?" If they want to remain anonymous, have them type it, print it, then leave it on your desk when you are not around.

Ask Your Team
for 360 Degree Feedback

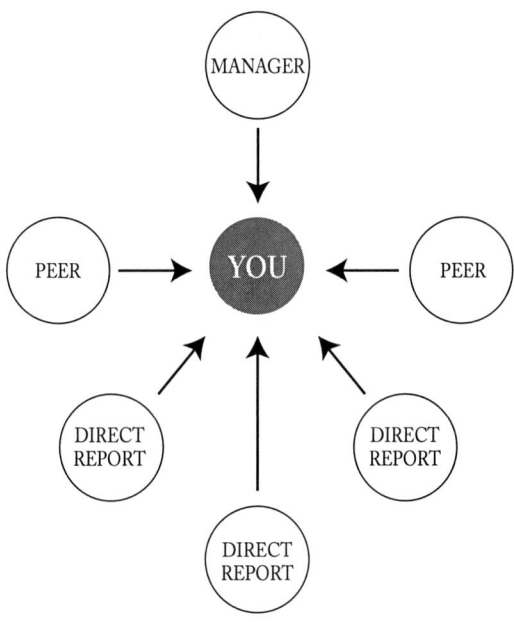

For more information on 360 assessments for you and your team, go to our website: **www.clearwater-consulting.com**

CHAPTER 3: Poor Leadership

Who do you respect? List ten people you can ask for feedback.

TOUGH TALK – Ten Tips for Disarming Difficult Conversations

"Everything that irritates us about others can lead us to an understanding of ourselves."

Carl Jung

Vision without execution is hallucination.

Thomas Edison

DIFFICULT CONVERSATION #4
Lack of Career Advancement

What happens to career advancement in the muck and mire of a sluggish economy or when senior level managers decide to work a few more years? How do you have the conversation with your boss or with Human Resources about your next steps and opportunity for development and advancement when there appears to be no path?

Consider evaluating next steps and your own professional growth from the perspective of overall career development—whether you stay at this company or move to another or start your own. Key to the conversation, whether you have it with your current HR department, or when interviewing elsewhere, is clarity about your vision for yourself.

One of our clients, Anna, a mid-level manager at an international technology company confronted that reality. She heard us speak at a workshop on executive presence and approached us with questions about what she specifically could do to strengthen her position within the company, so that when jobs became open, she would be competitive.

Regardless of whether Anna stayed at that IT company or moved on to another, she needed to strengthen her skills and her value through training and practice. She became a champion for the Clearwater Consulting Leadership Development Learning Forum, a 12-month series focused on key skills for mid-level managers. Through the monthly calls, fieldwork, articles and reports, and self assessments, the participants (limited in number) glean insight into their strengths and work on enhancing areas needing development.

Two "wins" for Anna emerged from this experience. First, since she was the initial advocate for the program in her company, her manager and peers saw her as a leader: someone identifying a need and introducing a smart solution. Second, she was a disciplined participant, making use of the material, the group coaching calls, her own self reflection to create a powerful personal development plan which she shared with her boss. This involvement effectively enrolled him in her success.

> Create a powerful personal development plan to be competitive when an opportunity is presented.

TIP #4

Articulate your vision for career development

A vision is a condition that is imagined, a future state that inspires you and others to achieve a higher level of excellence.

- How far down the road do you look and plan? A day, a week, a few months, a year, five years?

- Can you articulate a vision for yourself, for your development?

- Do you have a vision for your department or company?

- How clearly do you set direction for yourself and your team?

- How well have you planned out your next steps?

What is your vision for the next step in your career development? And what will be the impact on your department or company?

CHAPTER 4: Lack of Career Advancement

When you depersonalize abrasive behavior and see it as a call for help you become a catalyst for the best kind of change.

Marilyn Suttle

DIFFICULT CONVERSATION #5
Confronting Abrasive Behavior

In our work on cultural alignment, we spend a significant amount of time helping create team agreements. These are behaviors that the group commits to upholding.

When teams establish strong norms for positive interaction in a safe environment built on trust, it is much easier to call out behaviors that derail the team and its productivity.

A few of these derailers include

- Gossip or triangulation – talking about another person to a third party without ever addressing the core issue with the other person;

- Sarcasm that gets its bite at another's expense;

- Blame – the finger pointing behavior in an organization where each person or department is out for itself;

- Defensiveness – the classic response to real or perceived threat of blame;

- Arrogance – when confidence tilts over into know-it-all behavior, effectively leaving others feeling dismissed or inferior;

- Aggressiveness – when a blunt style becomes intimidating, there is a bully in the room.

> Abrasive behavior can derail the productivity of a team.

TIP #5

Name it

The simple act of identifying a derailing behavior allows you and your teammates to choose whether and how to address it. When we ignore or gossip about behavior that disrupts, we simply escalate its negative impact. When we set expectations—what we will and what we will not tolerate for example—everyone is clearer about the culture we collectively want to create and, together, build the norms that guide interactions.

There are two parts to this tip:

> First, name the agreements by which you and your teammates are willing to work together productively. For example, all voices count and are heard, celebrate successes, show up on time, invest in the team.

> Second, talk about how you each will call out derailing behaviors, such as those listed above, as inappropriate. Establish commitment to building the skill of direct confrontation.

Suggestions for how to approach one another when a derailer behavior appears:

- Remove emotion from your delivery;
- Factually share what you are noticing—patterns of behavior, concerns for negative impact, why it matters to you;
- Remind them of the team agreements.

Susan Scott, author of *Fierce Conversations*, gets it right with "The problem named is the problem solved" for without the ability to courageously name it, the action needed to resolve it cannot be taken.

What agreements are important to you?
What derailing behavior have you been tolerating?
What action can you take today to strengthen agreements and/or address derailers?

You gain strength, courage and confidence by every experience in which you must stop and look fear in the face.

Eleanor Roosevelt

Personal branding is the combination of one's skills and talents to produce value for people that creates an impression, a perception and reputation in the mind of others.

Bernard Kelvin Clive

DIFFICULT CONVERSATION #6
Executive Presence

According to a recent survey of professionals, executive presence accounts for 26% of the criteria considered for promotions.[9] There are many factors that contribute to a sense of someone's executive presence—confidence, authenticity, expertise, grace under fire, sharing a clear vision. Closely related to a sense of someone's executive presence is the person's brand—what they stand for, what they represent, and how consistent they are in their delivery, the perception that you can count on them and have confidence in them. So you see how the term executive presence starts to bridge to other attributes such as authority, authenticity, integrity, and trust.

There are several difficult conversations we encounter around executive presence. The most obvious potential derailer to the positive perception of executive presence is physical appearance. How do you tackle the tough question with a direct report or peer who repeatedly shows up inappropriately dressed? In your cultural setting, what is the norm? What is encouraged, tolerated, not tolerated? As a boss, the difficult conversation is striking the balance between encouraging someone to be authentic to their own personal style, and laying out the logic that for them to make a positive impression on others in the organization, their attire and physical presence cannot be off-putting. In most settings, clothing that does not fit well, is too tight, or is not clean sends a signal that the person does not care about himself, or, by extension, the job. Sometimes we see a newly promoted manager may fail to notice it is time to upgrade the wardrobe in keeping with the audiences he or she now needs to engage with—the board, the senior team, customers.

Another potentially difficult conversation related to executive presence points to presentation skills and how we engage the audience, which has implications for how we are perceived in terms of influence and impact.

In 2012, Amy Cuddy, Harvard social psychologist, shared with *Wired* magazine: "I noticed in class that women tended to make themselves small, holding their wrist, wrapping their arms around themselves. Guys tended to make themselves bigger. They're leaning back, stretching out, draping their arms around chairs. We know from studies of facial feedback that if you smile, you fake yourself into feeling happier. We wondered whether just asking people to spread out would help them feel more powerful, and it did." [10]

CHAPTER 6: Executive Presence

When dealing with a lack of confidence, try the Wonder Woman solution. Recent research by Dr. Cuddy pointed to the power—perceived and real—of emulating Wonder Woman: standing tall, with hands on hips. When the pose is held for a few minutes before going into a meeting, levels of testosterone increase while levels of cortisol (known as the stress hormone) decrease. [11]

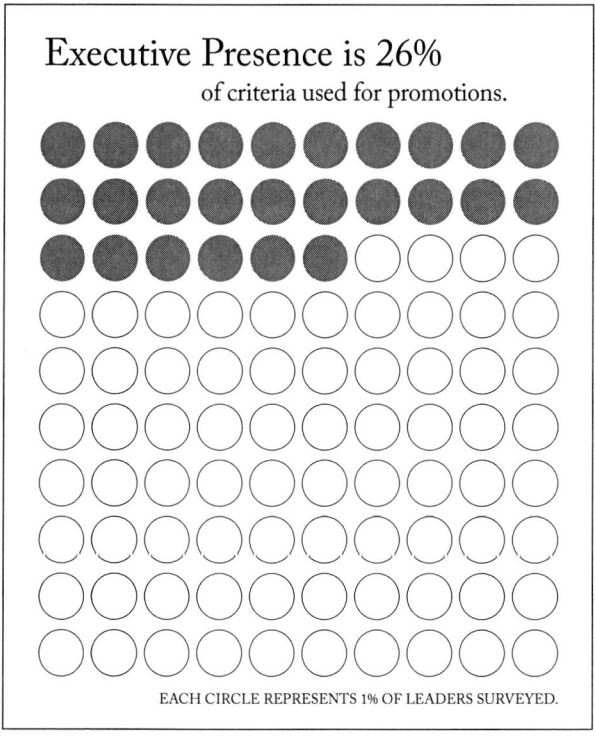

TIP #6

Take a Stand

Before talking to the person who has yet to fully engage with his or her executive presence, determine which of the following elements of presence seem to be the greatest area of concern. Which of these elements can you coach or counsel the individual to embrace? And before having the conversation, be aware of your own elements of executive presence: for each area, are you a role model?

- Create a positive impression
    - Physical appearance
    - Poise under fire
    - Approachable
- Engage and Enroll Others
    - Tactical skill of speaking clearly
    - Articulating your vision
    - Sense of vulnerability reflected in being open minded and open hearted
    - Setting clear expectations
    - Understanding your audience

- Show Commitment
    - Confident and self-assured
    - Credible
    - Accountable
    - Decisive
    - Passionate
    - Integrity

For a downloadable worksheet to help you assess your own executive presence go to:
www.clearwater-consulting.com/executive-presence-self-assessment

> Physical appearance, confidence, authenticity, expertise, grace under fire, and sharing a clear vision all contribute to executive presence.

What elements of your own executive presence need improvement?

CHAPTER 6: Executive Presence

One key to successful leadership is continuous personal change. Personal change is a reflection of our inner growth and empowerment.

Robert E. Quinn, Judge

DIFFICULT CONVERSATION #7
Change Resistant

How to fail when having this conversation: begin with "If only you would …"

Delete this sentence from your vocabulary. It implies many not very flattering things about the other person: that she has missed the obvious action (how dumb can she be!) or that he is interfering with your success (I can't succeed because you keep doing/not doing xyz!).

Change, though challenging, is possible and it is essential. If you are reading this book, you have committed to self-development, to learning, to applying new ideas. Those are some of your values. Part of disarming difficult conversations is taking a moment to understand the values the other person holds. Therein lays a secret to grasping why some people resist new ideas more than others.

One of the frameworks we use to explore resistance to change on a team or in an organization is the DISC work style. Its neutral approach to defining different work styles brings insight to other's motivations and helps defuse the potential conflict. The original assessment was created in the 1920s by William Marston, an interesting renaissance man. He developed one of the first lie detectors, and, with a group of other creative people, invented the comic book, Wonder Woman. During the era of Freud and discussions about how to categorize disease or mental illness, Marston was fascinated by how to categorize the behavior of normal people.

The evolution of his work has produced a profile called DISC. The one we use for individuals, teams and organizations is produced by the Wiley Company.

There are four primary DISC styles, all defined by specific and measurable behaviors:

 DOMINANCE

Interacts with his environment by being direct, decisive, results oriented, taking authority, skeptical and questioning, solving problems.

CHAPTER 7: Change Resistant

INFLUENCE

Engages with others through influence;
prefers solving problems with others versus alone
or relying exclusively on data; very collaborative,
enthusiastic and optimistic.

STEADINESS

Values security, consistency, loyalty;
wants to create a sense of stability and a
sense of safety so others feel comfortable
with each other and the direction taken.

CONSCIENTIOUSNESS

Approaches problems analytically, asks a lot
of questions in order to get to root cause,
is initially more skeptical than accepting
but can be won over by logic and data.

Each work style has a unique relationship to change. As a general rule, the greatest opportunity for change-resistant workers comes from the S and C quadrants. And the most proactive change agents in an organization will likely be D's and I's, both of whom are typically enamored of "what's new, what's next."

S's, who value stability and safety, get very attached to making the current situation or processes work. They defend the status quo. If change needs to occur, S's need advance warning, and a healthy understanding of the end goal. When they see where the group is headed and understand why, they can buy in and then play the role of being loyal to the leader in charge of change. They do not like surprises or explanations that only skim the surface. They want to be included in the discussion, and then, they can embrace the direction. Of all the profiles, S's will avoid conflict or disagreements, so resistance most often appears as silence and lack of engagement.

C's may resist change for a different reason. They value precision, accuracy, facts, understanding the pros and cons. If they cannot see with clarity the logic flow for a choice, they will resist, both indirectly (not showing up for meetings) or directly ("that's a really bad idea"). They may persist in criticizing the new approach until they buy into its value to the organization.

Another difference between the profiles is comfort with ambiguity. D's and I's inherently want to move toward resolution and are more comfortable not having all the facts. The pace set by C's and S's prior to acting is inherently more thoughtful and slower (thus frustrating the D's and I's), looking for information or interactions that clarify any ambiguity prior to decisive action.

TIP #7

Know your work style and priorities, and know theirs

- For more information on using DISC as a leadership tool and to help you and your team appreciate diverse styles, visit our website at:
  www.clearwater-consulting.com

> Understanding the values of the other person goes a long way toward disarming a difficult conversation.

Which DISC profile is most like you? And what are the implications for your communication regarding difficult conversations?

CHAPTER 7: Change Resistant

Never ruin an apology with an excuse.

Benjamin Franklin

DIFFICULT CONVERSATION #8
Apologizing

Patrick Lencioni, guru of team functionality (*The 5 Dysfunctions of Teams, The Advantage*) points to a willingness to apologize to one another as a team trait that positively correlates with productivity and team success. The more vulnerable the team members, the more unguarded, the more frequently they ask each other for input, the stronger the team and its outcomes.

Yet sharing our weaknesses or admitting mistakes is a difficult conversation for most of us.

What is so hard about admitting a mistake? And what is even harder about apologizing?

We are hired for our expertise. We are trained to be right. We have few really good role models for admissions of error.

Above and beyond the offenses of leaving someone off a routing list, or not responding in a timely fashion to an email, there are serious times when you need to bite the bullet to mend relationships that have been casualties of your own indifference or passion. Recall our client, Tom, from the chapter on poor leadership? Once he acknowledged his habit of taking credit without acknowledging the work his team or peers did, he chose to meet individually with each person he had affronted. In each case, they met off-site and he personally apologized for his behavior with specifics and real humility. He later shared with his Clearwater Consulting coach that this experience was one of the most exhilarating things he had ever done at work, truly a game changer for him.

> Willingness to apologize positively correlates with productivity and team success.

CHAPTER 8: Apologizing

TIP #8

Practice saying and meaning "I am sorry."

Identify some of the ways you might have blown it and practice how you might recover:

- I am sorry for leaving you off the routing list. That must have made you feel that you weren't a valued member of the team. I've added you to the routing list and hope you can make the next meeting on Monday.

- I am sorry I misinterpreted your silence as agreement. What do you really think about the decision?

- I am sorry I ignored your twenty emails. I would not have wanted you to do that to me. Truth is, I am overwhelmed by the amount of communication required on this project and I need to figure out another way to handle it. How do you do it?

- I'm sorry for not recognizing your contribution to the project during the meeting. That was a major mistake on my part and not only will it not happen again, but I've sent a follow up memo to everyone in the meeting apologizing for not recognizing your work and the work of the entire team.

To whom do you need to apologize today? What relationship needs repair?

CHAPTER 8: Apologizing

To whom should you apologize?

TOUGH TALK – Ten Tips for Disarming Difficult Conversations

Kindness is a language which the deaf can hear and the blind can see.

Mark Twain

To hold someone accountable is to care about them enough to risk having them blame you for pointing out their deficiencies.

Patrick Lencioni

DIFFICULT CONVERSATION #9
Peer-to-Peer Accountability

Clarify. Encourage. Confront. Own. Partner. Respond.

All of these verbs relate to the art of accountability: specifically, being able to respond appropriately to a colleague. Most of the time we wait for a team leader to handle lack of performance or an accountability issue. But when peers engage with each other to stay focused on the goal, the roles, and the timeframes, then team success soars and no one is waiting for the leader to save the day.

Most teams, according to Lencioni's Online Team Assessment, are terrible at it—nearly two-thirds of the 12,000 teams participating in the survey score in the lowest category for accountability.[12]

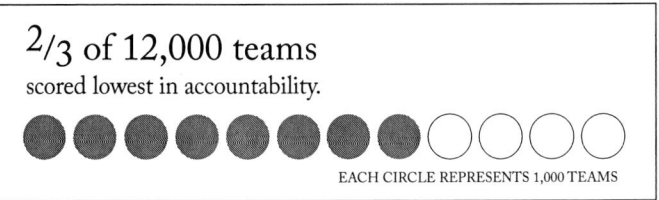

Much like the word "feedback," accountability has garnered a negative definition in business settings—suggesting that someone is not fulfilling a commitment.

What about holding myself accountable? What if you are a procrastinator, delaying delivery of a product, or project until you know it is perfect? How can I hold myself responsible and ask my teammates or colleagues to do the same in a way that will create positive momentum versus a negative environment?

When projects or work is initiated with clear goals and roles, accountability becomes an agreement between colleagues, a lynchpin for interactions and productivity, for support and encouragement. Not only do I agree to do xyz, but I agree that you have the responsibility to call me out when my work is less than great or not on time, and the responsibility to support me when I need help, as I will do for you.

There is an element of accountability that requires me to be vested in your success. If I'm not, then the interaction easily dissolves into finger pointing and blame (see Chapter 5 on Confronting Abrasive Behavior).

The other component we see lacking with teams in terms of accountability is having no process for handling disagreements or challenges. If by tacit consent everyone waits for the team leader to address situations, then the collective peer group is not responsible.

In most cases, the emotional underpinnings that precede the difficult conversation when a teammate or colleague appears to let you down exacerbates the already negative situation: the fact that work is not being accomplished. You feel betrayed, angry, frustrated. On the other hand, when accountability is defined and practiced as an ongoing tribute to shared accomplishment, to caring about the team outcomes as a whole, not just your piece of it, then we observe that teams catch misalignments and miscommunications or missed steps earlier in the process.

> Accountability becomes an agreement between colleagues with clear goals and roles.

TIP #9

Go First

It is much easier to confront a challenging situation requiring tough talk when you know what you are responsible for, what role others play, and what milestones along the way help define the path. Pick a project you are working on right now:

- **Clarify** each person's role and contribution, starting with your own.

- Make a public statement showing your **commitment** to the success of the project. Invite others to do the same.

- Who needs **encouragement**? What successful milestones can you celebrate now?

- **Confront** what is not working whether that is an individual behavior, a set of systems, lack of clarity. Set time aside to go through the facts of the situation. One fact may be that a member of the team simply does not have the skill necessary to contribute. Or that the team leader has not championed the appropriate resources the team needs.

CHAPTER 9: Peer-to-Peer Accountability

- **Own** your contribution to where things went off the rails.
- **Partner** with your peers and other resources to identify solutions.
- **Respond** to the situation without delay. Revisit the clarity of the project/program to be sure that next steps, roles, responsibility and commitments are clear.

What can you do to champion better peer-to-peer accountability with your team? What gets in the way? What is one step you can take today?

CHAPTER 9: Peer-to-Peer Accountability

*By failing to prepare,
you are preparing to fail.*

Ben Franklin

PREPARING FOR A DIFFICULT CONVERSATION
Putting It All Together

This chapter offers a deeper dive into the process of preparing for a difficult conversation. It will be easier to do if you have already worked through the previous nine tips, but even if not, it creates a framework you can use in advance of any conversation.

In a recent survey Clearwater Consulting conducted, the respondents overwhelmingly agreed that taking time before the conversation to think through the issues, to put one's self in the other's shoes, and to imagine the direction you want the conversation to go significantly enhanced the conversation and contributed to a positive outcome. Particularly when dealing with a difficult personality (the #1 issue our respondents identified), preparation is critical.

It is clearly the word to the wise—neither delay nor rush into a difficult conversation. Success depends upon your insights about the situation, about yourself, and the other person. It also depends upon your willingness to explore things with the other person that you may not have thought

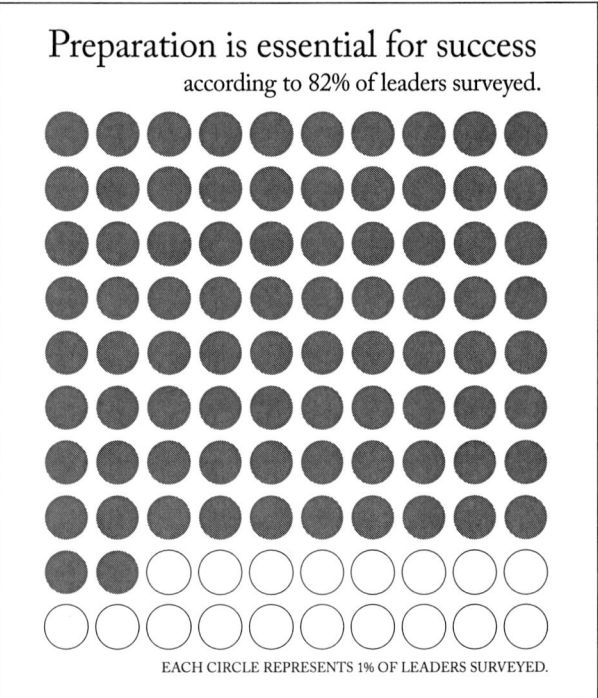

of in advance. Preparation is not about creating a script you follow. Rather, preparation focuses on having a framework before you approach the other person. Having a framework decreases your anxiety while your confidence in reaching resolution increases. The framework we suggest involves four parts: know your audience, know yourself, understand the situation, and know where you want the conversation to go.

CHAPTER 10: Preparing For A Difficult Conversation

To download a preparation worksheet, go to our website: **www.clearwater-consulting.com/preparing-to-have-a-difficult-conversation-at-work**

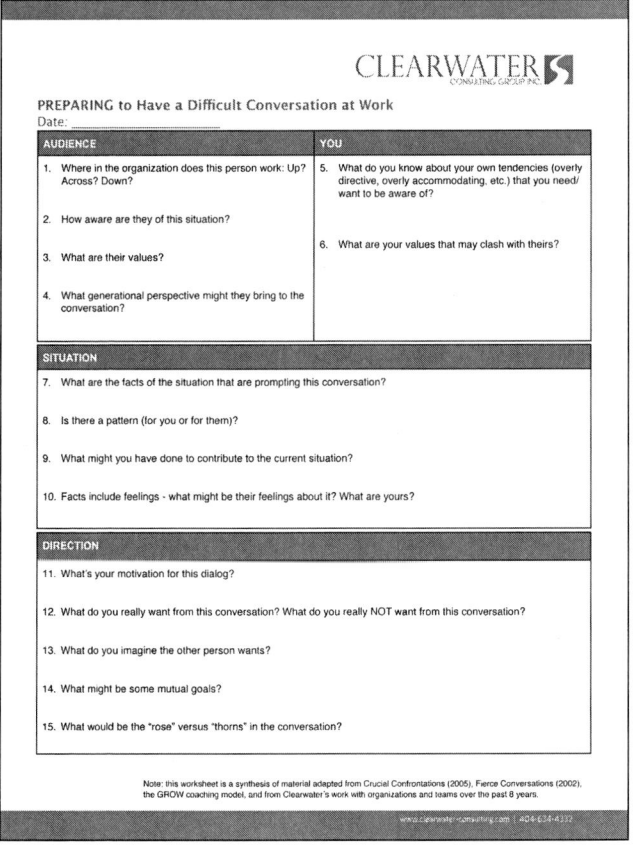

TIP #10

Be Prepared

I. Know Your Audience

Questions to ask yourself:

> a. What is your organizational relationship to them: are they a superior, peer, direct report, customer/client or vendor?
>
> b. Are they aware of the situation?
>
> c. What do they value?
>
> d. What is their work style or profile? If you are familiar with the DISC assessment, are they more action oriented or more thoughtful? Do they tend toward more engagement with people or with data?

Take as an example that you are preparing for a conversation with your manager. The topic has to do with how frequently your manager dumps a request on your desk without giving enough clarity or establishing priorities. This could fall into the "poor leadership" or "negotiation" category.

First, get clear about this individual—what facts do you know about him? What does he value: speed, thought-

CHAPTER 10: Preparing For A Difficult Conversation

fulness, collaboration, independence, sharing, doing? We point to values because more times than not, a situation has become dicey because one or both individuals believe the other is not valuing something dear to her. If I value punctuality and control over process and exploration, and you consistently show up late for meetings, I will soon be very frustrated. If you value ideation and creativity, you place less emphasis on schedules and do not understand why I am so distressed when you finally appear halfway through a meeting.

Managing 'up' is one of the most challenging skills to acquire. Having a difficult conversation with a superior is probably one of the most anxiety-producing experiences you will have at work. The difficulty may be prompted because you have bad news to share; or because you are asking the superior for more resources or clarity about your career path or you want a raise; or because you do not agree with direction as set. When the person is unaware of a situation or has a blind side regarding the topic, then an especially tough setting awaits. But, knowing that in advance helps you gauge how much time up front you need to share with her some helpful background and help her start to see the issues clearly. Regardless of what is prompting the conversation, consider that your chances for a successful outcome depend to a great extent on the value you bring to the conversation. Do you have suggestions for solutions to the problem identified? Are you willing to open yourself up to their input and ideas?

II. Know Yourself

First question: on a scale of 1 to 10, with 1 being no challenge at all and 10 being painfully challenging, just how challenging is this conversation going to be for you? The more challenging, the more preparation you will need.

Second question: on a scale of 1 to 10 with 1 being unimportant and 10 being top priority important, how important is this conversation to you? Without the motivation based on perceived importance of a conversation, it is challenging to gear up for it and to actually go through with it.

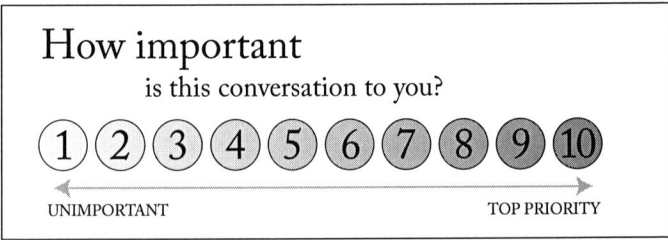

Are you a procrastinator? If you are in the huge percentage of people who delay the inevitable, make a commitment

CHAPTER 10: Preparing For A Difficult Conversation

to tackle the difficult conversation sooner rather than later. The amount of time it will free up for you—free from worry, anger, frustration, anxiety, and insomnia—and the clarity it will bring to your communication and interactions are well worth the discomfort up front.

What do you know about your own tendencies when working with others—do you tend toward being very directive, or overly accommodating? Share all the details, or get to the bottom line? What are your values and which of these might clash with theirs?

Back to the example of speaking with your manager: let us say you value stability, knowing what is coming, knowing why you are being asked to do something. In contrast, your manager is the poster child for speed—quick decisions and action. He likes bullet points, not paragraphs. He wants results, not discussion. He gets impatient with delay. You, on the other hand, get frustrated by not understanding the big picture; by not having enough information to feel informed so that you can appropriately respond.

How might you approach him about this topic? He cares about results, so you focus on how you can be more productive. He is interested in the bottom line so you share three points up front and refrain from getting carried away with too many examples.

III. Describe the Situation

Describe the situation in factual terms (avoid using "always" and "never"). Stick to facts that can be confirmed, not hearsay. For the other person, is this a pattern of behavior? Likewise, for you, is this a pattern? What might you have done to contribute to the current situation? What is the outcome of their behavior: positive and/or negative?

Facts include feelings. How might the other person be feeling right now? Put yourself in their shoes. What are your feelings? It is best to acknowledge them so they do not come screaming out in the middle of the conversation.

Try not to get stuck in the story here. In our example, the situation might be described like this: For the past three months, I have been given a new project every week with no prioritization or schedule. I feel frustrated because I am not doing my best work. I see that my boss is under tremendous pressure to launch these new projects among other things he is working on and I know he wants to succeed in order to impress the new president of the company. I am not the only one who is challenged by this lack of clarity and the increasing work load. I am worried we will not succeed nor be able to sustain this pace.

> Preparation is critical.

IV. Choose a Direction

In an ideal setting, what would be the outcome of this conversation? What is your motivation for the dialog? To prove you right and them wrong? To clear the air? To discover the underlying problems causing the situation? Or to find resolution?

What do you really want from this conversation and what do you NOT want from it? You want resolution. You do not want to escalate the pain. But sometimes resolution comes from vocal disagreement.

When talking with other person, it can be very helpful to say, "What I want from this conversation is for us to come up with a solution that enables us to get the work completed and allow for time to do our best work. What I don't want is to make this a complaint session (win/lose) situation."

Can you imagine what the other person wants? Reflect on his values and work style from previous interactions with him and imagine the ideal outcome from his perspective. Are there goals the two of you share? Imagine what those are and what success would look like.

In our example, let us say that the direction or outcome you want is help from your manager in prioritizing projects. Focus on what you need in order to succeed, and what success would look like for your boss. You may walk into the conversation with a proposed set of priorities as well as scheduling milestones and ask for his input. Ideally he will agree to provide clearer direction with the next new project—but if he does not offer this solution, you need to ask for it. It's a matter of your success and his (shared goal).

> *"The person who can most accurately describe reality without laying blame will emerge the leader."*
>
> Susan Scott

CHAPTER 10: Preparing For A Difficult Conversation

What do you need to work on—understanding the audience, understanding yourself, getting a better sense of the situation, or the direction you want the conversation to take?

TOUGH TALK – Ten Tips for Disarming Difficult Conversations

After more than forty years in business, I've concluded that listening is the single most important on-the-job skill that a good manager can cultivate.

J.W.Marriott, Jr

*Out beyond ideas of
rightdoing and wrongdoing,
there is a field.
I will meet you there.*

Rumi

TOUGH TALK
Conclusion

We all want a workplace in which we and our colleagues are engaged in productive work, a culture in which we identify and discuss issues as they occur, truthfully and with resolution, to work with others we trust and who trust us. But less than half of those recently surveyed believe their organization has such a candid environment in which those conversations can safely occur.[13]

What role can you play in creating safety and also in tackling the tough topics as they occur? Success in developing strong working relationships within your team and throughout your organization rests on your self-awareness. What do you need to work on and what relationships might you need to repair? What skill can you rely on and what wisdom can you share?

Tackling the challenge that, if allowed to fester, becomes nearly insurmountable takes courage and resolve. Find a

coach to support you. Raise the topic with your team and commit to developing the foundational skills that create success for you and your teammates.

No matter what your position within the organization, you play a role in creating a culture in which directness, candor, problem solving and resolution can occur.

CONCLUSION

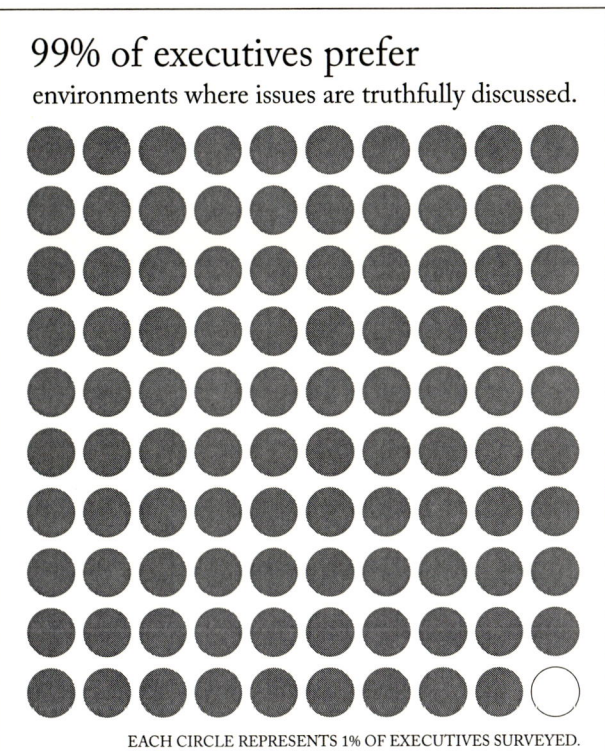

> Be proactive. Be bold.
> Be prepared. Go first.

*In the middle of difficulty
lies opportunity.*

Albert Einstein

TOUGH TALK
Endnotes

1. In its ongoing research to track difficult conversations, Clearwater Consulting Group finds that the need is pervasive: at any point in time in our survey results anywhere from 70 to 80% of responders are grappling with the need to have a challenging conversation.

2. Jennifer Ludden, *Ask For A Raise? Most Women Hesitate* (blog), January 08, 2011, www.npr.org/2011/02/14/133599768/ask-for-a-raise-most-women-hesitate.

3. Barbara Annis, and John Gray, *Work With Me*, (New York: Palgrave Macmillan, 2013), 94.

4. CEB, "Breakthrough Performance in the New Work Environment." 2012, 8-9.

5. Kerry Patterson, "Why Employees Fail to Change," *Talent Management Magazine*, November, No. 5, (2013).

6. Salary.com contributing writer, "Most People Don't Negotiate Due to Fear & Lack of Skills." Salary.com.

7. Vicki Slavina, *Why Women Must Ask (The Right Way): Negotiation Advice from Stanford's Margaret A.Neale* (blog), June 17, 2013.

8. Neale, Margaret. Stanford Business School, "Negotiation." Accessed January, 2014. www.leanin.org/education/negotiation.

9. Hewlett, Sylvia Ann, and et al. "Executive Presence." *Center for Talent Innovation*, 2012, 1.

10. Danielle Venton, *Power Postures Can Make You Feel More Powerful* (blog), May 05, 2012, www.wired.com/wired-science/2012/05/st_cuddy/.

11. Cuddy, Amy. TED Talk, June 2012. www.ted.com/talks/amy_cuddy_your_body_language_shapes_who_you_are.html.

12. Patrick Lencioni, *The Advantage*, (John Wiley & Sons, 2012).

13. Fierce Inc., "6 Key Trends That Increase Employee Productivity and Engagement." 2011. Page 6: Trend 4: People appreciate candor, yet do not see enough of it. 99% prefer a workplace in which people identify and discuss issues truthfully; 44% believe their organization has a candid environment

*Smooth seas do not
make skillful sailors.*

African Proverb

www.clearwater-consulting.com
404-634-4332

DEVELOPING LEADERS WHO DELIVER RESULTS
Clearwater Consulting Group

About Us

The consulting firm of Clearwater Consulting Group is focused on implementing leadership development strategies to help executives, teams, and organizations deliver exceptional results. Our unique offerings for leaders include programs designed for training Fortune 1000 leaders in navigating difficult conversations, developing extraordinary leadership, accessing coaching skills, inspiring teams, and enhancing executive presence. More than 2,500 leaders worldwide have used our training, coaching, and team facilitation services to develop their leaders and improve their commitment and engagement to their organizations.

Our Area of Focus

- **Leadership Development Training Topics**

  - **Great Manager Program**: 60 day program designed specifically for mid-level managers, coaching, feedback, leadership assessment and manager's matrix are the central components.

  - **Leader as Coach**: 90 day program designed to increase coaching capacity of mid and senior level executives. Listening, asking questions, and gaining perspective skills are emphasized and the GROW model is used to support coaching process.

  - **Enhancing Executive Presence**: a 2 hour, half-day or full day program designed to assess executives' understanding of their executive presence as it relates to communication style, confidence and appearance.

  - **Extraordinary Leadership Development**: a half-day, full day or 6 month long program focusing on delivery of extraordinary leadership skills—owning a vision, fostering belief, building a powerful network, commanding communication, and terrific team skills. Longer program includes executive coaching, assessments and cohort project.

- **Stepping into a Bigger Game at Work**: a half-day or full day format designed to call forth innovation, ingenuity and passion in leaders of organizations fostering greater vision, inspiration and teamwork from those they lead.

• **High-Functioning Team Development**

- **Annual or Bi-Annual Team Retreat**: can be customized for new teams, product launches, sales teams' annual sales goals and new leaders of teams with major agendas. Works best as a repeatable experience for the team to build greater accountability and commitment.

- **DISC 2 Hour Team Communication Workshop**: our basic team offering focusing on team profile, team style and team communication. Addresses the need for having all styles on teams and fosters agility in approach with different styles for optimal communication among team members.

- **Team Foundation Half-Day Training**: Program will start with DISC for enhanced relationships and creating buy-in among team members, layer in team agreements, team derailers and team commitments for an introductory program for building team positivity and productivity.

- **Team Development Acceleration**: 90 day program designed to work directly with the team leader to speed performance by building relationships, tackling change, overcoming dysfunction and measuring results. Two in-person full day retreats will be coupled with interviews with all team members, the coaching of the team leader and the real work application of solving problems to improve a team's performance.

• **Executive Coaching**

- **One-on-one coaching**: our coaching programs involve feedback and input from the coachee's leader, a consistent time and place for executive coaching with the coachee either by phone or in-person, a process for navigating the on-going programmatic assignment and a final action plan for sustainable action after the assignment concludes.

- **Leadership Development Learning Forum**: many of our tailored leadership development topics require on-going work and support for skill acquisition and lasting change. For some mid-level leaders, the best place to acquire these skills is in a coaching cohort program. Attendees sign up for 6-month or year-long programs and calls/webinars are led and facilitated by Clearwater Consulting trained coaches. Learning is pragmatic, actionable and fun. Pricing is accessible based on group format.

- **On-boarding the new leader**: It is no secret that 40-50% of all new leaders—whether they are from the inside or outside of an organization—fail. For this reason, Clearwater Consulting's 3–6 month on-boarding program is all about creating the vision, navigating the culture, accelerating real wins and building a network, to optimize a leader's timeline to success.

- **360 feedback and coaching**: Clearwater Consulting can leverage a company's 360 assessment or deliver one of a company's choosing. Because our coaches are certified in a plethora of 360 feedback tools and have delivered many different types of 360 feedback debriefs and coaching sessions, this area of real core competency results in enhanced leadership self-awareness and capacity.

Our Approach

The Clearwater Consulting approach in working with a variety of industries (including technology, health care, pharmaceutical and retail) and over 2,500 leaders in development of leadership skills is based on best practices in adult learning models. We balance interactive training and experiential learning with real work examples for practical and immediate applications.

Our customized programs incorporate the phases of **Discovery** through interviews and assessments of leaders and stakeholders, out of which we then **Design** a customized curriculum and approach to address particular situation or goal, **Delivery** of the work in workshops, senior team offsites, and executive coaching of senior leaders, **Debrief** to discuss how to sustain the application of the lessons, insights and continuing accountability and finally **Declare** ways to sustain the learning by accessing on-demand follow-up content, curriculum, and coaching. Traditional lecture style with PowerPoint presentations are replaced with thought-provoking, insightful exercises, modules and discussions, so the experience becomes one of problem solving and creative interaction with real world applicability and sustainable follow through.

Our Team

Our exceptionally skilled, customer-focused consultants pride themselves on their ability to create environments (inside organizations) of exceptional learning where true leadership development happens.

For more detailed individual bios, please visit our website: **www.clearwater-consulting.com**

Principals

Andrea Hopke, Co-Principal, is expert in designing and delivering team development and leadership programs that increase engagement, build bench strength, and accelerate an executive's vision. With a master's degree in social psychology she helps clients understand the social dynamics of groups and the role they can play in driving positive results in an organization during times of change. Andrea is gifted at clearly assessing the current situation and then developing unique content and approaches. Her work resonates across managerial levels within an organization and across a variety of industries, including healthcare, technology and retail. A superior facilitator and systems thinker, with decades of experience co-leading several services organizations in consulting and strategic research, she brings a practical approach to the real work of implementing sustainable solutions.

andrea@clearwater-consulting.com

Becky Dannenfelser, Co-Principal, brings over 25 years of stellar success at Macy's both as an active leader, guiding individuals and teams repeatedly to positive results, and as a founding member of the Federated Leadership Institute and the Leadership Advisory Council for High Potentials. Her enthusiasm, dedication and passion for positive change fuel the work she does with executives at all levels. She understands the needs of today's leaders in Fortune 500 companies, having led divisions of $350 million to $1 billion and having personally grappled with the myriad challenges all leaders confront. She role models the quote by Tom Peters "Leaders don't create followers, they create more leaders." Becky is driven to support the individual leader, the team, the organization to step up to its vision of success through leadership at all levels.

becky@clearwater-consulting.com

Partners

Alison Valli, Senior Partner. She has over 20 years of experience in leading and developing top-performing organizational teams within the retail industry, both at Macy's/Federated and May Department Stores where she most recently led the $280 million Women's Accessories division of Macy's Central. Her consistent track record of sales performance, combined with her MBA in HR and Finance, offers clients a role model of a leader who has regularly achieved award-winning performances for both revenue and profit in a Fortune 500 company.

alison@clearwater-consulting.com

Conni Todd, Senior Partner. She brings 20+ years of progressive sales experience to her role as senior partner and corporate coach. Her award-winning sales leadership as a multiple President's Club Winner combined with her track record of consistent results offers clients focused attention on managing internal and external customer relationships while driving results. Designated as high potential during her career with AT&T, Conni offers a balanced perspective of organizational challenges with the development and retention of rising stars.
conni@clearwater-consulting.com

Laura Stanley, Senior Partner. Her past experience as a human resources executive with over 20 years of talent management and strategic human capital experience, combined with her international MBA, offer clients a unique view of the employer/employee perspective and the best ways to successfully engage an organization's talent. Laura's background includes roles with recruiting at Korn/Ferry International and evolved into senior human resources leadership positions at EarthLink and EzGov, Inc., with a focus on talent acquisition and talent management.
laura@clearwater-consulting.com

Shirley Wulf, Senior Partner. She has over 26 years of sales leadership and management experience with a major Fortune 500 pharmaceutical company. Shirley was one of the first female leaders promoted into a major sales leadership role and she blazed a trail that allowed many other women a track record of success. As partner to Clearwater Consulting clients, Shirley blends her vast industry knowledge and experience in sales leadership development and sales team effectiveness along with her certifications in coaching and leadership development to showcase real world experience that gets results.

shirley@clearwater-consulting.com

TOUGH TALK
About the Authors

Andrea and Becky have been business partners, friends and allies for nearly ten years. They feel incredibly fortunate to work with each other and to have the opportunity to act as trusted advisors to courageous clients willing to stretch beyond comfort zones.

This is their first book, gleaned from the hands-on experiences of growing a business, guiding clients, and witnessing first-hand the positive impact of mastering difficult conversations.

Becky lives in Atlanta, Georgia, with her charming husband, two talented teenaged sons, her saint of a mother, and their affectionate dog. Andrea and her handsome husband live in Decatur, Georgia, with two loving cats.

Becky Dannenfelser
and Andrea Hopke

www.clearwater-consulting.com
404-634-4332

Human beings love to be right. When a person is willing to give up being right, a whole world of possibilities opens up.

Pete Salmanson

Thank you for reading
Tough Talk.

Contact Clearwater Consulting Group
if we can help you, your team, or your
organization learn more about successfully
disarming difficult conversations.

For access to resources, webinars, and other
materials to strengthen your skills, go to:
www.clearwater-consulting.com/books/toughtalk

www.clearwater-consulting.com
404-634-4332